Christianity, Democracy, and the American Ideal

Jacques Maritain
(1882-1973)

Christianity, Democracy, and the American Ideal

A Jacques Maritain Reader

Compiled and edited
by James P. Kelly, III

SOPHIA INSTITUTE PRESS®
Manchester, New Hampshire

Sophia Institute Press®
Box 5284, Manchester, NH 03108
1-800-888-9344
www.sophiainstitute.com

Excerpts from the following works by Jacques Maritain are reprinted with the
kind permission of the following rights holders:

Education at the Crossroads: Yale University Press; Copyright © 1943 Yale Uni-
versity Press. *Man and the State:* University of Chicago Press; Copyright © 1951
The University of Chicago. *On the Use of Philosophy:* Princeton University
Press; Copyright © 1961, 1989 Princeton University Press. *Ransoming the Time:*
Charles Scribner's Sons; Copyright © 1941 Charles Scribner's Sons; copyright
renewed © 1969 by Jacques Maritain; reprinted with the permission of Scribner, an imprint of Simon & Schuster Adult Publishing Group. *Reflections on
America:* Charles Scribner's Sons; Copyright © 1958 Jacques Maritain; re-
printed with the permission of Scribner, an imprint of Simon & Schuster Adult
Publishing Group. *Some Reflections on Culture and Liberty:* University of Chicago Press; Copyright © 1933 The University of Chicago.

Library of Congress Cataloging-in-Publication Data

Maritain, Jacques, 1882-1973.
    Christianity, democracy, and the American ideal : a Jacques Maritain
reader / compiled and edited by James P. Kelly, III.
      p. cm.
    Includes bibliographical references and index.
    ISBN 1-933184-01-9 (pbk. : alk. paper)
    1. Democracy — Religious aspects — Christianity. 2. Christianity and
politics — United States. I. Kelly, James P., 1956- II. Title.

BR115.P7M3363 2005
261.7'0973 — dc22   2004026680

The editor wishes to thank
Sally and Frank Hanna, III
and
Kim and David Hanna
for their friendship and support

Contents

�

Introduction

For centuries, the Christian faith has served as a foundation for democracy. Individuals who rely on gospel values to guide their private and public lives make good citizens. They focus on things above the earth as well as on it and thereby are more likely to reject the materialism and moral relativism that undermine the common good.

Regrettably, many leaders in western democracies reject this fact.

Jacques Maritain, one of the great moral and political philosophers of the twentieth century, wrote and spoke extensively about the threats that secularism, materialism, and coercive social engineering by state authorities pose to human persons and to the democratic experiment. This book contains some of Maritain's prophetic thoughts. It shows how, until recent times, the Christian faith has shielded America from these destructive tendencies, and it suggests how it can begin doing so once again.

Respect for the dignity of the human person was paramount for Maritain. In his view, the dignity of each "single human soul" reaches its full expression in each person's freedom to enter into a direct relationship with God, who creates the order of naturally sacred things.

Maritain argues that freedom defined as individual license undermines the dignity of the person, a condition that has been aggravated by recent decisions of the U.S. Supreme Court which declare that abortion and homosexual conduct are constitutionally protected fundamental rights.

According to Maritain, modern democratic governments have "yearned to enslave man" by implementing social, educational, and legal policies that encourage a separation between God and humanity. In particular, he insisted that science and technology be subordinated to a religious ethic and serve a higher morality. Current debates over bioethics, including the ethics of human cloning and embryonic-stem-cell research, show that the need for such subordination is greater than ever.

Maritain understood that it was through a direct and intimate relationship with God that individuals receive what he called the "energies of spiritual and social resurrection" so essential to democracy. He viewed God as the end of the human person and the prime source of political society. His views are directly relevant to the debate over whether the Ten Commandments may be posted in public places, including schools, courthouses, and public grounds.

For Maritain, gospel values are compatible with the common good, and the grace of Christ is the means for realizing those values. But grace does not come cheaply. Maritain shows that "heroism of the plain man" is required to live in accordance with the gospel.

This is especially so in modern society, where politically and culturally engaged Christians often encounter resentment and discrimination in the public square. In spite of such treatment, Christian leaders concerned about the issues of life, family, and marriage have embraced Maritain's challenge to awaken the people to the need for political action.

Most education leaders understand the importance of gospel values and other peace-loving religious values to the building of the common good; however, they emphasize a technical, utilitarian education that does little to instruct children in how to handle their personal freedom responsibly.

Maritain saw "education at the crossroads" in regard to the modern conflict between education for social utility and education for freedom. He was particularly concerned about the government assuming responsibility for the moral education of children. His concern is legitimate, as public-school educators have embraced a full-fledged character-education dogma designed to inculcate children in an essentially secular ethic having no transcendent dimension.

Due, in large part, to the devastating effects of secularism in America, lay Christians have recently embraced a multitude of ministries designed to heal the bodies and souls of those in need. In many instances, these ministries, referred to by Maritain as "little teams and small flocks," have followed his prescription that they make private vows of prayer a central element in their missions.

Yet Maritain anticipated the modern tendency of a paternalist state to usurp the vital role traditionally played by faith-based and community organizations. To counter that tendency, he was one of the first to call for the decentralization of social life in favor of what he referred to as a "personalist and pluralist" regime. In such a regime, the state would provide all nonviolent faith-based and community organizations with equal access to government social service, health, and education grants. Maritain's prophetic ideals have been realized through the recent expansion of government support for faith-based and community initiatives.

Unfortunately, financial cooperation between the state and faith-based organizations is hindered by a false interpretation of the Establishment Clause of the United States Constitution that perpetuates the myth that there must be an absolute separation of church and state. From Maritain's perspective, freedom of thought, religion, and association are imperative, and the state should not fund policies that inhibit the beneficial practice of "free men speaking to free men." In conformity with Maritain's principles, numerous public-interest law firms have recently been formed to protect the free speech and religious liberty of individuals and faith-based organizations.

Although Maritain called upon Christians to become more active in the work of democracy, he placed equal emphasis on the need for Christians to be "humble stars invisibly shining" by means of contemplation of the demands of the Christian life and on God as the source of truth and love. Maritain's equal concern for the vertical movement of man toward God and the horizontal movement of man through history arose from his concern about the degree to which modern democratic societies tempt individuals to abandon the pursuit of truth in favor of the pursuit of material wealth.

Maritain also understood that contemplation and prayer are critical to the Christian social mission to "exist with the people" by suffering with them. He was particularly moved by the manner in which, consistent with the Christian redemptive experience, the "bruised souls" of poor immigrants are transformed into a source of new strength and new hope for America.

Because of his belief in the uniqueness of the human person and in religion as the guiding factor in a person's relationship to others, Maritain expressed frustration over those who were willing to sacrifice truth in pursuit of human fellowship. Although he was an early and influential participant in the formation of the United Nations and its subsidiary bodies, Maritain cautioned against those leaders who, sacrificing truth for human fellowship, advocated the practice of "kneeling before the world." In his view, the pursuit of human fellowship should not be politicized by highlighting those human values and rights that facilitate economic development or population control while undermining those human values and rights that protect and promote traditional interpersonal and family relationships. Maritain would be concerned over the United Nations' current promotion of a human-rights-education agenda in primary and secondary schools designed to impose a global secular religion that conflicts with the moral views of many families.

Ultimately, although he was concerned about the progress of humanity, Maritain had no utopian aspirations. For him, the primary calling of the Christian is to intervene in the destiny of the world, "to have been present," acting on history to the limit of our power.

To the limit of his own power, Jacques Maritain was present to help humanity comprehend the proper relationship between Christianity and democracy, particularly in the context of the American experience. The lessons in this book show how we can continue his presence by using his wise ideals to improve American society and our global community.

Christianity, Democracy, and the American Ideal

Chapter One

~

"A Single Human Soul"

Democracy of the Person

Throughout his life, Maritain expressed the need for an integral humanism that considered man not as a merely material individual, but as a person having both natural and supernatural ends. A person concerned about his supernatural aspirations will exercise his free will in a way pleasing to God. The gospel encourages and gives strength to those who aspire to show love, justice, and respect for others; thus, Christianity helps preserve and protect democracy by enabling people to live and work together in peace. To flourish, modern democracies must reject materialism and individualism in favor of such a personalist, integral conception of life and society.

~

Faith in the dignity of the human personality, in brotherly love, in justice, and in the worth of the human soul outweighing the whole material universe — faith, in a word, in the conception of man and his destiny which the gospel has deposited at the very center of human history — this faith is the only genuine principle by which the democratic ideal may truly live. Any democracy that lets this faith be corrupted lays itself open to that extent to disruption.

☞

A person is a universe of spiritual nature endowed with freedom of choice and constituting to this extent a whole that is independent in face of the world; neither nature nor the state can lay hold on this universe without its permission. And God Himself, who is and acts within, acts there in a particular manner and with a particular exquisite delicacy, which shows the value He sets on it. He respects its freedom, at the heart of which He nevertheless lives. He solicits it; He never forces it.

☞

A single human soul is of more worth than the whole universe of bodies and material goods. There is nothing above the human soul except God. In the light of the eternal value and absolute dignity of the soul, society exists for each person and is subordinate thereto.

The worth of the person, his liberty and his rights, arise from the order of naturally sacred things, which bear upon them the imprint of the Father of being, and which have in Him the goal of their movement. A person possesses absolute dignity because he is in direct relationship with the absolute, in which alone he can find his complete fulfillment.

Christianity confirms and emphasizes the concrete sense of equality in nature by affirming its historical and genealogical character, and by teaching that here we are concerned with a blood relationship, properly so-called — all men being descended from the same original parents, and being brothers in Adam before they are brothers in Christ. The *unity of mankind* is at the basis of Christianity.

The American body politic is the only one that was fully and explicitly born of freedom, of the free determination of men to live together and work to-gether at a common task. And in this new political

5

creation, men who belonged to various national stocks and spiritual lineages and religious creeds — and whose ancestors had fought the bitterest battles against one another — have freely willed to live together in peace, as free men under God, pursuing the same temporal and terrestrial common good.

⁊

This freedom is not a celestial condition received once and for all, and to be simply enjoyed. Existing in history, and being a human thing — a most precious and lofty, and therefore, endangered, human thing in the realm of civilization — it is perpetually threatened by new obstacles and perils arising from new situations in the process of time. It must be perpetually defended and improved; it must be a new conquest and creation for each generation. It permits no inertia, no passivity, no rest. It must be unceasingly regenerated by the life-breath of a free people, and so it is one with this very life-breath.

⁊

This freedom leads to the discovery of a more profound and real sense of the dignity of the human person. As a consequence, man would rediscover himself in God and would direct social work toward a heroic ideal of fraternal love. Such a humanism, which considers man in the integrality of his natural and supernatural being and which sets no prior limits to the descent of the divine into man, could be termed the *humanism of the Incarnation*.

᷒

In brief, the question is to know whether, in fact, in the historical development of humanity, a slow work is not being performed, a slow and spontaneous activation of human conscience and conduct, tending to bring humanity closer to an order, of which democracy of the individual was but a counterfeit; which I call *democracy of the person*. And the question is also to know whether this democracy of the person is possible only with the superelevation that civilizations receive from the energies of Christian life.

᷒

Modern democracies suffer from a philosophy of life that undermines and annihilates from within their vital principle. If they are to rediscover a sense of justice, and of risk, and of heroism, it is under the condition of rejecting their materialist philosophy, and of viewing in full light a personalist conception of life and of society.

☞

For Further Reading and Reflection
Maritain Sources

On the rights of man: *Man and the State*, pages
76-107.

On human equality: *Ransoming the Time*, pages 1-32.

On natural law and the rights of the person: *The Rights
of Man and Natural Law*, pages 50-114.

Church Documents

On the dignity of the person: Pope Paul VI's *Gaudium
et Spes* (On the Church in the Modern World, 1965),
paragraphs 14-22.[1]

On the value and absolute dignity of human life:
Pope John Paul II's *Evangelium Vitae* (The Gospel
of Life, 1995), paragraphs 2-4, 7, 18-23, 34, 69-71,
87, and 96.

[1] Most of these Church documents can be found online at
the Vatican website: www.vatican.va.

⁀

Chapter Two

"They Yearn to Enslave Man"
The Limits of Social Planning

Men desire peace; however, as the last four centuries have revealed, pure reason has failed to produce a "scientific" creed uniting men in peace. Maritain respects the important roles of science and social planning; nevertheless, unless science is subordinated to a religious ethic, humanity is lost. Social planners have attempted to substitute centralized techniques and a secularized common good for a Christian philosophy that respects the creative spiritual energies of each person. Similarly, politicians have subordinated spiritual ends to political ends. Later in his life, Maritain lamented the burden imposed on the people of modern Europe by a scientific — as opposed to integral — humanist philosophy of life.

⁀

In modern times, an attempt has been made to base the life of civilization on the foundation of

mere reason — reason separated from religion and
from the gospel. This attempt fostered immense
hopes in the last two centuries, and rapidly failed.
Pure reason has appeared less capable than faith
of ensuring the spiritual unity of mankind, and the
dream of a "scientific" creed uniting men in peace
and in common convictions about the aims and
basic principles of human life and society has
vanished in contemporary catastrophes.

⌒

Nevertheless, I disapprove of those who wish
to suppress scientific advances. But if science and
technology are not mastered and subjected force-
fully to human good — that is to say, entirely and
rigorously subordinated to a religious ethic and
rendered instruments of a higher morality — then
humanity is lost.

⌒

The very expression "common faith" should
make us realize that democratic inspiration cannot
find in "scientific method" its highest source of
authority. This "faith" is "of a secular not supernatural character"; yet even a secular faith implies the
commitment of the whole man and his innermost

spiritual energies, and draws its strength, therefore, from beliefs that go far beyond scientific method, being rooted in the depths of each individual's options and personality.

☞

It is hard to imagine a *culture* organized and unified by social planning alone — even supposedly intelligent social planning. Such a cultural paradise would offer, I am afraid, little chance for the creative powers of human personality as well as for the enthusiasm and happiness of the people.

☞

The fact remains that democratic faith — implying as it does faith in justice, in freedom, in brotherly love, in the dignity of the human person, in his rights as well as in his responsibilities, in that power of binding men in conscience which appertains to just laws, in the deep-rooted aspirations that call for the political and social maturity of the people — cannot be justified, nurtured, strengthened, and enriched without philosophical or religious convictions (whether theological, metaphysical, or naturalistic) that deal with the very substance and meaning of human life.

In the course of twenty centuries, by preaching
the gospel to the nations and by standing up to the
flesh-and-blood powers to defend against them the
liberties of the spirit, the Church has taught men
freedom. Today the blind forces that for two hundred years attacked her in the name of freedom and
of the human person deified are at last dropping
the mask. They appear as they are. They yearn
to enslave man.

We thus perceive the state of tension and conflict that human society inevitably involves. Social
life is naturally ordained — in the measure in which
I have tried to define — to the good and to the
freedom of the person. And yet there is in this very
social life a natural tendency to enslave the person
and to diminish him, insofar as this person is considered by society as simply a part and as simply a
material individual.

The truth is that Europe has forgotten the subordination of political to spiritual ends. There lies its

great mistake. Hence derives that general condition of the oppression of the spirit and the conscience; that contempt in practice for human personality and its dignity, the overwhelming burden of which is everywhere more or less consciously felt.

⌒

For Further Reading and Reflection
Maritain Sources

On the rejection of Christianity by modern democracies: *Christianity and Democracy*, pages 25-32.

On the nature of the democratic charter: *Man and
the State*, pages 108-146.

On the implications of atheism on modern society:
The Range of Reason, pages 103-117.

On the secularization of modern society: *The Range
of Reason*, pages 185-192.

On the anti-Christian forces in modern society:
The Twilight of Civilization, pages 9-38.

Church Documents

On the devastating results of the attempt to base the life
of civilization on reason separated from religion and
the gospel: Pope John Paul II's *Fides et Ratio* (Faith
and Reason, 1998), paragraphs 16-18, 31-33, 45-46,
62-63, 73-74, 80-81, 86-93, 101-102, and
106-107.

꙳

Chapter Three

"Energies of Spiritual and Social Resurrection"

Christianity and the Common Good

For Maritain, the common good is a living, evolving ideal that is maintained and advanced by the creative spiritual energies of individual citizens. Conversely, unjust and immoral political acts harm the common good. A democratic government must positively cooperate with all the diverse religious groups constituting political society to promote the virtues of justice and friendship. Thus, a government policy of absolute strict separation between church and state is a counterproductive one. Worse, a government policy that expressly rejects God as the prime source of political society is a destructive one. Regarding such policies, the present debates over issues such as the public funding of faith-based initiatives, the posting of the Ten Commandments in public buildings, and the removal of the word God from the Pledge of Allegiance are instructive.

≈

The aim of society is its own *common good*, the good of the social body. But if we failed to grasp the fact that this good of the social body is a common good of *human persons*, as the social body itself is a whole made up of human persons, this formula would lead in its turn to other errors — of a collectivist type, or to a type of state despotism.

≈

Justice and moral righteousness are essential to the common good. That is why the common good requires development of the virtues in the mass of citizens, and that is why every unjust and immoral political act is harmful to the common good.

≈

The point is that right political experience cannot develop in people unless passions and reason are oriented by a solid basis of collective virtues: by faith and honor and thirst for justice. The point is that without the evangelical instinct and the spiritual potential of a living Christianity, political judgment and political experience are ill-protected against temptations born of selfishness and fear;

without courage, compassion for mankind, and the
spirit of sacrifice, the advance toward a historical
ideal of generosity and fraternity is not conceivable.

☙

The democratic philosophy of man and society
has faith in the inherent goodness and mission of
human nature. In the great adventure of our life
and our history, it is placing its stakes on justice and
generosity. It is therefore betting on heroism and
the spiritual energies.

☙

We have no illusions about the misery of human
nature. But we have no illusions, either, about the
blindness of the pseudo-realists who cultivate and
exalt evil in order to fight against evil, and who
consider the gospel a decorative myth that we could
not take seriously without throwing the machinery
of the world out of order.

☙

To rise above the fatal policies of totalitarianism,
we need an awakening of liberty and its creative
forces; we need the energies of spiritual and social
resurrection — of which man does not become

capable by the grace of the state or any party peda-
gogy, but by a love that fixes the center of his life
infinitely above the world and temporal history.

☞

The conception of society we are describing recognizes that, in the reality of things, God, principle
and end of the human person and prime source of
natural law, is by the same token the prime source
of political society and authority among men. It
recognizes that the currents of liberty and fraternity released by the gospel, the virtues of justice
and friendship sanctioned by it, the practical respect for the human person proclaimed by it, and
the feeling of responsibility before God required
by it are the internal energy civilization needs to
achieve its fulfillment.

☞

In this conception, civil society is organically
linked to religion and turns consciously toward
the source of its being by invoking divine assistance
and the divine name as its members know it. Independent in its own temporal sphere, society has
above it the kingdom of things that are not Caesar's,
and it must cooperate with religion, not by any

kind of theocracy or clericalism, nor by exercising any sort of pressure in religious matters, but by respecting and facilitating on the basis of the rights and liberties of each of us, the spiritual activity of the church and of the diverse religious families that are grouped within the temporal community.

꩜

If one day there is to exist here below a truly universal civilization; that is to say, one founded — no matter how strong its internal differences — on first common principles, and recognizing in an organic and actual manner the same common good, it will have risen higher, in its own order, by the influence of energies whose source is the grace of Christ.

꩜

In the perspectives of integral humanism, there is no occasion to choose, so as to sacrifice one or the other, between the vertical movement toward eternal life (present and actually begun here below) and the horizontal movement whereby the nature and creativity of man are revealed in history. These two movements should be pursued at the same time.

Christianity, Democracy, and the American Ideal

For Further Reading and Reflection
Maritain Sources

On the relationship between Christianity and democracy: *Christianity and Democracy*, pages 42-74; *The Twilight of Civilization*, pages 39-47.

On the nature of Christian political action: *Integral Humanism*, pages 256-271; *Scholasticism and Politics*, pages 154-178.

On the nature of Christian or "integral" humanism: *Scholasticism and Politics*, pages 1-19; *The Range of Reason*, pages 192-199.

On the relationship between the person and society: *Scholasticism and Politics*, pages 45-70; *The Person and the Common Good*, pages 37-79; *The Rights of Man and Natural Law*, pages 1-43.

Church Documents

On the call for the spiritual renewal of Europe: Pope John Paul II's *Ecclesia in Europa* (The Church in Europe, 2003), paragraphs 6-16, 19-20, 24-27, 46-49, 58-60, 67-69, 78-79, 84-85, 97-99, and 108-121.

Chapter Four

⁓

"The Heroism of the Plain Man"

Courage and Democracy

Maritain's vision of integral humanism contemplates a heroic attitude on the part of citizens and the state. For the citizen, a willingness to make sacrifices for the common good evidences an awareness of, and a desire to work toward, the rewards of eternal salvation. However, the sacrifices made by citizens yield a full harvest only in those instances in which the state similarly adopts the view that the vertical movement toward eternal life is as important as the horizontal movement of man through history. Only then will the state be prepared to risk everything for justice and love.

⁓

We don't believe Paradise will arrive tomorrow. But if we want civilization to survive, the task to which we are summoned, the task we have to

pursue with all the more courage and hope because
at each moment it will be betrayed by human weak-
ness — this task must have for its objective a world
of free men imbued in its secular substance by a
genuine and living Christianity, a world in which
the inspiration of the gospel will direct common
life toward a heroic humanism.

❧

When man accepts death freely — not as an
enslaved fanatic or blind victim, but as a man and a
citizen, for the sake of his people and his country —
in that very act of extraordinary virtue he affirms at
the same time the supreme independence of the
person in relation to the things of this world. In
losing himself, in a temporal sense, for the sake of
the city, the person sacrifices himself, in the most
real and complete fashion. Yet the person is not
defeated. The city still serves him because the soul
of man is immortal and because the sacrifice gives
grace one more chance.

❧

Those Christians who are turned toward the
future and who hope — even though it be a long-
range hope — for a new Christendom, a new

Christianity-inspired civilization, know that the
world has done with neutrality. Willingly or unwill-
ingly, states will be obliged to make a choice for or
against the gospel. They will be shaped either by
the totalitarian spirit or by the Christian spirit.
They know that a new Christianity-inspired civilization, if and when it evolves in history, will be not
a return to the Middle Ages, but a new attempt to
make the leaven of the gospel quicken the depths
of temporal existence.

If the Western democracies are not to be swept
away, and if a centuries-long darkness is not to
come down upon civilization, they must discover
in its primitive purity their vital principle, which
is justice and love, and whose source is of divine
origin. They must reconstruct their political philosophy and thus rediscover the sense of justice and
heroism in the rediscovery of God.

Nations that want to survive and live in peace
have to understand that neither of these two
goals is to be attained without clearly facing the
risk of war; it is only when the existence of this risk

has been acknowledged and accepted that it is possible to adopt a policy intelligent enough to obviate it. The European democracies understood this too late. Every democracy whose rule of life is not heroic but hedonistic will grasp such things too late.

⁂

We have the right to call, not for a continual outpouring of collective heroism, but for the common acceptance of an ideal of heroic life, upon the heroism of the plain man.

⁂

If the common life in which I am engaged is built upon injustice, one day I will have to look on with courage while the beasts skin me and my children alive. If common life tends toward justice, perhaps I ought to give up my skin and all the rest for justice: at least I shall have the expectation that my children will be happy, and courageous as well.

It is far better to run oneself ragged for the good than to run ragged for evil. These are simple facts; the time will come when the common conscience will understand them.

⁀

Will Christians finally resolve to understand
the proper law of Christian action? Or are they
ashamed to be called children of the light? The
question is not one of condemning or rejecting
the means of force and physical restraint, if justly
employed. It is rather a question of recognizing the
importance of those means founded on moral or
inner energy; on spiritual firmness; on personal
courage, risk, and suffering. It seems very remark-
able that in the great dictatorships with all their
power, a single man who can say, "I do not agree"
appears as an intolerable and extremely dangerous
enemy. Why, if there is not in conscience, honor,
truth, patience, and love a certain hidden strength
that the totalitarians fear?

⁀

What I mean is that it is not enough to define
a democratic society by its legal structure. Another
element plays also a basic part — namely, the dy-
namic leaven or energy that fosters political *movement,* and which cannot be inscribed in any
constitution or embodied in any institution, since
it is both personal and contingent in nature, and

rooted in free initiative. I should like to call that existential factor a *prophetic* factor. Democracy cannot do without it. The people need prophets.

⌒

The people are to be awakened; that means that the people are asleep. People as a rule prefer to sleep. Awakenings are always bitter. Insofar as their daily interests are involved, what people would like is business as usual: everyday misery and humiliation as usual. People would like not to know that they are *the* people. It is a fact that, for good or evil, the great historical changes in political societies have been brought about by a few who were convinced that they embodied the real will of the people — to be awakened — in contrast with the people's wish to sleep.

⌒

In the reality of existence, the world is infected with lying, injustice, wickedness, distress, and misery; creation has been corrupted by sin to such an extent that in the very marrow of his soul, the saint refuses to accept it as it is. Evil — I mean by that the power of sin, and the universal suffering that it drags in its wake — is such that the only thing the

saint has immediately at hand to oppose it totally is
to give everything, to abandon everything — the
sweetness of the world, and what is good, and what
is better, and what is delectable and permitted, and
more than anything, himself — to be free to be
with God. To do this is to be totally stripped and
given over in order to seize the power of the Cross;
it is to die for those he loves.

Christianity, Democracy, and the American Ideal

⌒

For Further Reading and Reflection
Maritain Sources

On the relationship between courage and democracy:
Christianity and Democracy, pages 89-98.

On the lack of political courage in France prior to
World War II: *France My Country*, pages 5-34.

On the nature of exemplary and unapparent saints:
Notebooks, pages 240-242.

On the favorable characteristics of Americans:
Reflections on America, pages 36-42.

Church Documents

On the courage necessary to fight the relativism, social
injustices, and other grave conditions present in
modern society: Pope John Paul II's *Veritatis Splendor*
(The Splendor of Truth, 1993), paragraphs 1, 2, 12,
15, 31-32, 42, 50, 83-108.

☞

Chapter Five

"Education at the Crossroads"

The Role of the State in Education

Maritain expressed concern over the proper goal of edu-
cation in a democracy, which, in his opinion, was to lead
citizens to spiritual freedom and to personal and social re-
sponsibility. He was especially concerned about the cleavage
in education between religious inspiration and secular
learning, of which the state's concentration on vocational
training and the teaching of secularized character education
are evidences. Parents are the primary educators of their
children, and the state's educative function is to help the
family fulfill this mission. By supporting the growing home-
school and school-choice movements in America, educa-
tion authorities serve that more limited and proper function.

☞

The sorrows and hopes of our time undoubtedly stem from material causes — economic and

technical factors that play an essential role in the course of human history — but even more profoundly, they stem from ideas, the drama in which the spirit is involved, the invisible forces that arise and develop in our minds and hearts.

≈

Nothing is more important than the events that occur within that invisible universe which is the mind of man. And the light of that universe is knowledge. If we are concerned with the future of civilization, we must be concerned primarily with a genuine understanding of what knowledge is: its value, its degrees, and how it can foster the inner unity of the human being.

≈

We may now define in a more precise manner the aim of education. It is to guide man in the evolving dynamism through which he shapes himself as a human person — armed with knowledge, strength of judgment, and moral virtues — while at the same time conveying to him the spiritual heritage of the nation and the civilization in which he is involved, and preserving in this way the century-old achievements of generations.

The Role of the State in Education

⁂

To have made education more experiential, closer to concrete life and permeated with social concerns from the very start, is an achievement of which modern education is justly proud. Yet, to reach completion, such a necessary reform must understand, too, that to be a good citizen and a man of civilization, what matters above all is the inner center, the living source of personal conscience in which originate idealism and generosity, the sense of law and the sense of friendship, respect for others, but at the same time deep-rooted independence with regard to common opinion.

⁂

If we remember that the animal is a specialist, and a perfect one, all of its knowing-power being fixed upon a single task to be done, we ought to conclude that an educational program that would aim only at forming specialists ever more perfect in ever more specialized fields, and unable to pass judgment on any matter that goes beyond their specialized competence, would lead indeed to a progressive animalization of the human mind and life.

☞

How could the common man be capable of judging about the good of the people if he felt able to make judgments only in the field of his own specialized vocational competence? Political activity and political judgment would become the exclusive job of specialized experts in the matter — a kind of state technocracy that does not open particularly felicitous perspectives either for the good of the people or for liberty.

☞

In an effort to compensate for the inattention to moral formation caused by overspecialized technical training, educational authorities have undertaken what is known as "education of will," "education of feeling," "formation of character," and so on.

☞

Character is something easily warped or de-based, difficult to shape. All the pedagogical hammering of nails into the shoe doesn't make the shoe more comfortable to the foot. The methods that change the school into a hospital for refitting

and vitalizing the will, suggesting altruistic
behavior, or infusing good citizenship, may
be well conceived and psychologically suitable,
but they are, for the most part, dishearteningly
ineffective.

꙰

As a result of the present disintegration of
family life, of a crisis in morality and the break
between religion and life, and finally of a crisis in
the political state and the civic conscience, there
is everywhere a tendency to burden education with
remedying all these deficiencies. This involves a
risk of warping educational work, especially when
immediate transformations are expected from its
supposedly magic power.

꙰

The state would summon education to make
up for all that is lacking in the surrounding order
in the matter of common political inspiration,
stable customs and traditions, common inherited
standards, moral unity and unanimity. It would urge
education to perform an immediate political task
and, in order to compensate for all the deficiencies
in civil society, to turn out in a hurry the type of

person who is fitted to meet the immediate needs of the political power.

⁀

Accordingly, education would become a function directly and uniquely dependent on the management of the state, and the educational body an organ of state machinery. As a result of the extraneous and unnatural burden thus imposed upon education, and of the subsequent annexation of the educational task by the state, both the essence and freedom of education would be ruined.

⁀

For just as man is constituted a person, made for God and for a life beyond time, before being constituted a part of the political community, so, too, man is constituted a part of family society. The end for which the family exists is to produce and bring up human persons and prepare them to fulfill their total destiny. And if the state, too, has an educative function, if education is not outside its sphere, this function is to help the family fulfill its mission and to complement this mission — not to efface in the child his vocation as a human person and replace it by that of a living tool and material for the state.

The Role of the State in Education

What is most important in the upbringing of
man — that is, the uprightness of the will and the
attainment of spiritual freedom, as well as the achievement of a sound relationship with society — is truly
the main objective of education in its broadest sense.

As regards the prospect for education in America, I also should like to say that no story is more
dramatic and hopeful, and testifies more strongly
to the greatness of men of goodwill, than the story
of the three hundred years of achievements here.
The democratization of education, and the discovery of educational ways and means better fitted for
the nature and dignity of the children of man, con-
stitute one of the glories of this country. Now it
seems that American education finds itself at the
crossroads. I am convinced that if it frees itself from
the background of an instrumentalist and pragma-
tist philosophy that is but a hindrance to its inspiration, and which takes the edge off the sense of truth
in our minds, this profoundly personalist and humanist educational venture will push forward with
renewed power.

⌒

For Further Reading and Reflection
Maritain Sources

On the proper aims of education: *Education at the Crossroads*, pages 1-28.

On the trials of education: *Education at the Crossroads*, pages 88-118.

Church Documents

On the Second Vatican Council's vision for Christian Education: Pope Paul VI's *Gravissimum Educationis* (Declaration on Christian Education, 1965).

On the fulfillment of the mission of Catholic universities and institutes of higher education: Pope John Paul II's *Ex Corde Ecclesiae* (On Catholic Universities, 1990), paragraphs 12-49. See also the United States Conference of Catholic Bishops' (USCCB) 1999 Application of *Ex Corde Ecclesia* to the United States[2] and the USCCB's 2001 Guidelines Concerning the Academic Mandatum in Catholic Universities (Canon 812).

---

[2] Copies of USCCB documents can be found online at www.nccbuscc.org.

⫘

Chapter Six

"Little Teams and Small Flocks"

Faith-Based Initiatives

Maritain believed that the person naturally tends to so-
cial life and communion. The highest forms of social life
are communities that come together in pursuit of essential
truths, and thereby radiate love. These communities real-
ize that, in spite of their religious inspiration, they must en-
gage the secular social and political order, as participants
and critics. Integral humanism requires that Christians,
through prayer and communion with other Christians,
gain the grace and energy necessary to live in the world.
Nevertheless, communities of faith must resist the tempta-
tion to link themselves so closely to a particular political
party as to surrender their independence in spiritual affairs.

⫘

The person is a whole, but he is not a closed
whole; he is an *open* whole. He tends by his very

nature to social life and to communion. This is true
not only because of the needs and the indigence
of human nature, by reason of which each of us has
need of others for his material, intellectual, and
moral life, but also because of the radical generosity inscribed within the very being of the person,
because of that openness to the communication
of intelligence and love which is the nature of the
spirit and which demands an entrance into relationship with other persons. To state it rigorously,
the person cannot be alone. He wants to tell what
he knows, and he wants to tell what he is. Whom
would he tell, if not other people?

⌒

From the family group, the person moves on to
civil or political society, and in the midst of civil
society it feels the need for more limited groups or
fellowships that will contribute to its intellectual
and moral life.

⌒

If we take all of the foregoing into account, it
clearly appears that it is more than ever the task of
little teams and small flocks to struggle for man and
the spirit, and in particular to give effective witness

to those truths for which men so desperately long and which are, at present, in such short supply. For only the little teams and small flocks are able to muster around something that completely escapes technique and the process of massification: the love of wisdom and of the intellect and the trust in the invisible radiation of this love.

⁀

Historically, the great fact is that [America] was born of politico-religious communities whose autonomous behavior, traditions, and self-government have left an indelible impression on the general mood of the American people. Hence, at the very time when the necessities of life and the extraordinarily fast growth of the American nation oblige it to increase more and more the powers of the federal state, the American mind still does not like the look of the very notion of *state*. It feels more comfortable with the notion of *community*.

⁀

If the considerations I have presented here are correct, those groups which would be founded on a sound political philosophy and a sound philosophy of modern history would apply themselves to a

political action *at long range*, which, instead of
hypnotizing itself on the present moment, would
reckon on *duration* and take into account the time
of maturation necessary for an integral humanist
renewal of the temporal order

☞

It seems normal, and inevitable, that to new
social and political conceptions there correspond
appropriate organs of action. The awakening of
Christian conscience to the strictly temporal, social,
and political problems implied in the inauguration
of a new Christendom will entail, I hold, the birth
of new temporally and politically specified political
formations, whose inspiration will be intrinsically
Christian.

☞

The new political formulations of which I am
speaking presuppose indeed a profound spiritual
revolution; they can come to existence only as
expressions of the resurrection of religious forces
that will take place in hearts. They presuppose also
a vast and multiform work of preparations, in the
order of thought and in that of action, of propa-
ganda, and of organization.

It seems to me that there is matter here for practical reflection. I mean that one can ask oneself if, in the present state of the world, it is not especially desirable to see develop groups of laymen which, while pursuing such or such particular goals (studies and progress in the intellectual life, professional improvement, works of mercy, social action, aid to underdeveloped countries, and so on), and while fully keeping their lay character, would have at their base a free gift to God whose seal and guarantee would be private vows bearing on certain requirements of Christian life and of the advance toward perfection.

Foremost among the private vows of which I speak would come the vow of prayer. For fidelity to prayer is for each a kind of spiritual equivalent of the cloister for the contemplative religious, and it is, according to all great spiritual teachers, the foundation of progress toward the perfection of love. And this fidelity, taking into account the practical possibilities of each, can be assured in lay life as well as in religious life — even if, in certain cases, it is only a quarter of an hour devoted to the silence of recollection, as St. Theresa said.

There have always been (and there will never be enough) centers of peace and of radiance in which men find a little silence to listen to God, and to join their energies with a view to what He can eventually inspire them to undertake. These centers are like portals through which the angels of Heaven steal invisibly among us. For centuries it was the monasteries and the religious houses that above all fulfilled this office, and they will not cease to fulfill it; and everything new that is tried will always need to go there to be reinvigorated.

Now, just as it is not particularly favorable, as a rule, for religion to be too much brandished about and made use of by the officials of any government, so the much deeper phenomenon of which I just spoke — temporalized religious inspiration in a nation or a civilization — however normal and salutary it may be in itself, involves its own accidental dangers. The risk is that *religion itself* might become temporalized; in other words, so institutionalized in the temporal structures themselves, and in the temporal growth of a given civilization, that it would practically lose its essential supernatural, supra-temporal, and supra-national transcendence, and become subservient to particular national or temporal interests.

☞

The temptation to link religion to some political party "of the left" is considerable for men eager to secure positive results, because the evils and injustices of the prevailing social system, against which the spirit of the gospel inclines us to fight, are also the most apparent object of the protests in which the tendencies "of the left" find their *raison d'être*.

☞

The temptation to link religion to some political party "of the right" is considerable for men of principles (when their principles are not sufficiently exalted), especially in times of disorder, because such parties are then, as it were, the memory of, and the permanent claim to restore, a state of public order that has disappeared.

The spiritual must free itself from the earthly fetters that threaten to enslave it. We must realize that, however important human and political means may be in the sphere of the temporal good, they are the least effective for the extension of the kingdom of God and that in proportion to the degree that the world falls to pieces, they will appear more and more inadequate in that sphere. We must realize that, however necessary any kind of political activity may be, it is confined to a particular human plane, where religion can make an authoritative intervention for the protection of the spiritual good; but it can never surrender its own independence.

⌒

For Further Reading and Reflection
Maritain Sources

On the formation and conduct of study circles and annual retreats by the laity: *Notebooks*, pages 133-185; 290-297.

On the Catholic Church and social progress: *Ransoming the Time*, pages 196-216.

On American lessons in political and social philosophy: *Reflections on America*, pages 161-191.

On the dangers of politicizing religion: *The Things That Are Not Caesar's*, pages 44-77.

Church Documents

On Maritain's vision for "little teams and small flocks": Pope John Paul II's *Christifideles Laici* (The Lay Members of Christ's Faithful People, 1998), paragraphs 1, 3-5, 16-17, 26-29, 40-44, and 58-60.

⌒

Chapter Seven

"A Personalist and Pluralist Regime"

Freedom of Association

*According to Maritain, states should adhere to the prin-
ciple of subsidiarity — the idea that larger and higher
organizations should not usurp functions that smaller and
lower bodies can perform more efficiently. The state should
create an environment that encourages multiple associations to arise for the pursuit of the common good. Eastern
Europe imploded over the repressive policies of a collectivist state; Western Europe is reeling from the depressive
policies of the welfare state. America is split between
those who look to the state to ensure economic parity and
social stability immediately and those who look to free associations to advance the common good over time.*

⌒

Whereas, for centuries, the crucial issues for
religious thought were the great theological

controversies centered on the dogmas of faith, the crucial issues now will deal with political theology and political philosophy.

⤢

The state is only that part of the body politic especially concerned with the maintenance of law, the promotion of the common welfare and public order, and the administration of public affairs.

⤢

The end of political society is not to lead the human person to his spiritual perfection and to his full freedom of autonomy; that is to say, to sanctity, to a state of freedom which is properly divine because it is the very life of God living in man. Nevertheless, political society is essentially destined, by reason of the earthly end that specifies it, to the development of those environmental conditions which will so raise men in general to a level of material, intellectual, and moral life in accord with the good and peace of the whole, that each person will be positively aided in the progressive achievement of his full life as a person and of his spiritual freedom.

⤢

Of course, there is for everything great and powerful an instinctive tendency — and a special temptation — to grow beyond its own limits. Power tends to increase power; the power machine tends ceaselessly to extend itself. The supreme legal and administrative machine tends toward bureaucratic self-sufficiency; it would like to consider itself an end, not a means.

⤢

How to describe this process of perversion? It occurs — that is apparent from all our previous remarks — when the state mistakes itself for a whole, for *the* whole of the political society, and consequently takes upon itself the exercise of the functions and the performance of the tasks that normally pertain to the body politic and its various organs. Then we have what has been labeled "the paternalist state": the state not only supervising from the political point of view of the common good (which is normal), but directly organizing, controlling, or managing (to the extent it judges the interests of public welfare to demand) all forms — economic, commercial, industrial, cultural; or dealing with scientific research as well as with relief and security — of the body politic's life.

☞

The fact remains that the state has skill and competence in administrative, legal, and political matters, but is inevitably dull and awkward — and, as a result, easily oppressive and injudicious — in all other fields. To become a boss or a manager in business or industry or a patron of art or a leading spirit in the affairs of culture, science, and philosophy is against the nature of such an impersonal topmost agency, abstract, so to speak, and separated from the mutual tensions, risks, and dynamism of concrete social existence.

☞

As a result, I would say that if our present social structure is to evolve along normal lines, a first step, made necessary by the requirements of public welfare, would consist in having the state start and support large-scale undertakings planned and managed *not* by the state and not from the center of the country's political administration, but by private enterprises coordinated with one another and by the various communities of the very people concerned, under the leadership of independent responsible appointees. Thus, the state itself would launch a movement of progressive decentralization and "destatization" of social life, tending toward the advent of some new personalist and pluralist regime.

⌐

The final step in such a new regime would take place when prodding by the state would no longer be necessary, and all organic forms of social and economic activity, even the largest and most comprehensive ones, would start from the bottom. By this I mean from the free initiative of and mutual tension between the particular groups, working communities, cooperative agencies, unions, associations, and federated bodies of producers and consumers, rising in tiers and institutionally recognized. Then a definitely personalist and pluralist pattern of social life would come into effect in which new societal types of private ownership and enterprise would develop. And the state would leave to the multifarious organs of the social body the autonomous initiative and management of all the activities that by nature pertain to them.

Christianity, Democracy, and the American Ideal

As opposed to the various totalitarian conceptions of political society in vogue today, the conception here is of a pluralist body politic bringing
together in its organic unity a diversity of social
groupings and structures, each of them embodying
positive liberties.

⌒

For Further Reading and Reflection
Maritain Sources

On a philosophy of freedom: *Freedom in the Modern World*, pages 5-41.

On the pluralist principle in democracy: *Integral Humanism*, pages 162-184; *The Range of Reason*, pages 165-171.

On the proper relationship between the people and the state: *Man and the State*, pages 1-27.

Church Documents

On the proper relationship between church and the political community: Pope Paul VI's *Gaudium et Spes* (On the Church in the Modern World, 1965), paragraphs 73-76.

On Maritain's concern for the principle of subsidiarity and the proper ordering of relationships between the state and voluntary associations created for economic, social, and other purposes: Pope John Paul II's *Centesimus Annus* (On the hundredth anniversary of Pope Leo XIII's *Rerum Novarum*, 1991), paragraphs 1, 10, 12, 13, 15, 25, 29, 44-49, and 58.

⤜

Chapter Eight

"Free Men Speaking to Free Men"

Freedom of Thought and Religion

There is no complete distinction between matters of governance and matters of faith, especially in America, where legislatures write laws and courts decide cases that bear on human life, health, marriage, the family, and education. Maritain held freedom of conscience to be a sacred right through which a person directs his life toward God. The state, although rightfully concerned with promoting a democratic charter expressing the virtues of the common good, should never compel citizens to ignore the dictates of their consciences in reaching such a consensus. In a democracy, diverse philosophical or religious schools of thought should freely compete in the construction of the democratic charter.

⤜

The Lord Christ said, "Render therefore to Caesar the things that are Caesar's: and to God, the things that are God's." He thereby distinguished the two powers and, in so doing, emancipated the souls of men.

☞

Any sort of temporal work — not only a public decree or legislative enactment, the raising of taxes, the declaration of war or a treaty of peace, but also the activity of a professional or syndical or political group, the exercise of some particular civic right — may come into special connection with the good of souls, once it becomes, for instance, the occasion of some spiritual aberration or happens to affect sufficiently seriously the rights and liberty of the Church or the orientation of the faithful toward eternal salvation.

Who is to be the judge of such a connection and of the gravity of the spiritual interests involved? Clearly the Church alone.

☞

As a Catholic and by my Catholic Faith, I am bound in conscience to no human, theological, or philosophical opinion, however well founded it may be, and still less to any judgments on contingent or worldly matters, or to any temporal power.

Nor am I bound to any particular form of culture or civilization, and still less of race or blood. I am bound uniquely to what is universality itself and super-universality: to the Divine, to the words and precepts of Him who said, "I am the Truth, I who speak to you."

~

The secret of the heart and the free acts thereof, the universe of moral laws, the right of conscience to hearken unto God, and to make its way to Him — all these things, in the natural as in the supernatural order, cannot be tampered with by the state nor fall into its clutches. Doubtless, law binds in conscience, yet this is because it is law only if just and promulgated by legitimate authority, not because the majority or the state can be the standard of conscience.

~

The body politic has the right and the duty to promote among its citizens, mainly through education, the human and temporal — and essentially practical — creed on which depend national communion and civil peace. It has no right, as a merely temporal or secular body, enclosed in the sphere

where the modern state enjoys its autonomous
authority, to impose on the citizens or to demand
from them a rule of faith or a conformism of reason,
a philosophical or religious creed that would present itself as the only possible justification of the
practical charter through which the people's common secular faith expresses itself.

⌒

As a result, it is but normal that in a democratic
culture and society, the diverse philosophical and
religious schools of thought which, in their practical conclusions, agree with regard to democratic
tenets, and which claim to justify them, come into
free competition. Let each school freely and fully
assert its belief! But let no one try to impose it by
force upon the others! The mutual tension that en-
sues will enrich rather than harm the common task.

⌒

There is no belief except in what is held to be
intrinsically established in truth, nor any assent of
the intellect without a theoretical foundation and
justification. Thus, if the state and the educational
system are to perform their duty and inculcate the

democratic charter in a really efficacious way, they
cannot help resorting — so that minds will be put
in possession of such a foundation and justification,
and perceive as true what is taught them — to the
philosophical or religious traditions and schools of
thought that are spontaneously at work in the consciousness of the nation and which have contrib-
uted historically to its formation.

☙

Adherence to one of these schools of thought
or another rests with the freedom of each person.
But it would be sheer illusion to think that the
democratic charter could be efficiently taught if
it were separated from the roots that give it con-
sistence and vigor in the mind of each one, and if
it were reduced to a mere series of abstract formu-
las — bookish, bloodless, and cut off from life.

☙

On the one hand, the state — or the groups
and agencies in the body politic that are concerned
with education, or the authorities that govern the
educational system — should see to it that the
democratic charter be taught (in a comprehensive,
far-reaching, and vitally convincing manner) in all

the schools and educational institutions. On the other hand, and for the very sake of fostering the democratic faith in people's minds, the educational system should admit within itself *pluralistic* patterns enabling teachers to put their entire conviction and most personal inspiration in their teaching of the democratic charter.

☞

The pluralism I am advocating for public schools should relate, in my opinion, not to the curriculum, but to the various inspirations with which the common curriculum would be taught if the members of the teaching body were distributed and grouped according to their own wishes, as well as to the moral geography of local communities and the requests of associations of parents. In this way, their own personal or philosophical convictions would roughly correspond to those that prevail in the social environment.

☞

The most rational solution, in tune with the pluralistic principle, would consist of having the teaching of the democratic charter given not by one, but by several teachers belonging to the main religious

or philosophical traditions represented in the stu-
dent population of a given school or college, each
one of those teachers addressing the students of his
own spiritual tradition. Yet as logical as it may be,
such a solution has little chance, I am afraid, to appear feasible to our contemporaries. Something else
should be carried into effect, in every country, to
ensure a real and efficient teaching of the democratic charter in public schools.

~

If a new civilization is to be inspired by Christianity, if the body politic is to be quickened by
the leaven of the gospel, it will be because Christians will have been able, as free men speaking to
free men, to revive in the people the often uncon-
scious Christian feelings and moral structures
embodied in the history of nations born out of
old Christendom, and to persuade the people, or
the majority of the people, of the truth of Christian
faith, or at least of the validity of Christian social
and political philosophy.

~

I would say, therefore, that in the matters we are
considering, civil legislation should adapt itself to

the variety of moral creeds of the diverse spiritual lineages that essentially bear on the common good of the social body — not by endorsing them or approving of them, but rather by giving allowance to them.

⁀

By removing obstacles and opening the doors, the body politic and its free agencies and institutions would positively facilitate the effort of the apostles of the gospel to go to the masses and share their life, to assist the social and moral work of the nation, to provide people with leisure worthy of human dignity, and to develop within them the sense of liberty and fraternity.

Such would be, as I see it, the positive cooperation between the body politic and the Church.

Freedom of Thought and Religion

⁀

For Further Reading and Reflection
Maritain Sources

On the relationship between church and state: *Man and the State*, pages 147-187; *The Things That Are Not Caesar's*, pages 1-43; 78-110.

Church Documents

On the relations between the Church and state in western democracies: Pope Paul VI's *Dignitatis Humanae* (Declaration on Religious Freedom, 1965).

Chapter Nine

"Humble Stars Invisibly Shining"
Contemplation and Prayer

The construction of the democratic charter is a job for con-
templative philosophers, not scientists and social planners.
For their part, Christian citizens are called to perfection
and the contemplation of the gospel and the saints. Focused
as it is on action rather than on contemplation, American
society can benefit from the contemplation and prayers of
Christians and others, particularly the contemplation of
charity. The more public-school authorities and courts re-
sist reasonable attempts to facilitate voluntary contempla-
tion or prayer by students, the less likely future Americans
will be to alter their materialistic, chaotic lifestyles.

☞

There is a certain number of moral tenets —
about the dignity of the human person, human rights,
human equality, freedom, law, mutual respect and

tolerance, the unity of mankind, and the ideal of peace among men — on which democracy presupposes common consent; without a general, firm, and reasoned-out conviction concerning such tenets, democracy cannot survive. It is not the job of scientists, experts, specialists, and technicians; it is the job of philosophers to look for the rational justification and elucidation of the democratic charter.

❦

Contemplation is a winged and supernatural thing, free with the freedom of the Spirit of God, more burning than the African sun and more refreshing than the waters of a rushing stream, lighter than birds' down, unseizable, escaping any human measure and disconcerting every human notion, happy to depose the mighty and exalt the lowly, capable of all disguises, of all daring and all timidity, chaste, fearless, luminous and nocturnal, sweeter than honey and more barren than rock, crucifying and beatifying (crucifying above all), and sometimes all the more exalted the less conspicuous it is.

❦

All, without exception, are called to perfection, which is the same as that of the Father who is in

Heaven; in a manner either close or distant, all are
called to the contemplation of the saints — not the
contemplation of the philosophers, but to loving
and crucified contemplation. All without exception. The universality of such an appeal is one of
the essential features of Christianity's *catholicity*.

⁖

We hold that the West will not surmount the crises in which it is engaged, unless it reconquers that
vital truth and understands that external activity
must overflow from a superabundance of internal
activity, by which man is united to truth and to the
source of being. If a new age of Christian civilization should dawn, it is probable that the law of
contemplation superabounding in action would
overflow in some way into the secular and temporal
order. It would thus be an age of the sanctification
of the profane.

⁖

And we ourselves know that we can deliberate
about ourselves, judge our own actions, cling to what
is good because it is good and for no other reason;
all of us know more or less obscurely that we are
persons, that we have rights and duties, that we

preserve human dignity within ourselves. Each of us can, at certain moments in his existence, descend into the innermost depths of the ego, to make there some eternal pledge or gift of himself, or face some irrefutable judgment of his conscience; and each of us, on such occasions, alone with himself, feels that he is a universe unto himself, immersed in, but not dominated by, the great star-studded universe.

⌒

To my mind, if, in American civilization, certain elements are causing complaints or criticisms, those elements proceed definitely from a repression of the desire, natural in mankind, for the active repose of the soul breathing what is eternal.

⌒

The modern world has completely reversed that essential order of human life. Exterior activity began three centuries ago and more to absorb the whole life of man, because, in reality, the world then turned to the conquest and practical utilization of matter away from union with God through faith and love. Conversion to perishable goods, the definition of mortal sin, gradually became the general attitude of civilization.

⁀

What is it, as a matter of fact, to live a truly Christian life, if not to strive, each according to his condition, for Christian perfection; that is to say, for the perfection of charity? The first thing needed by the world is the contemplation of the saints and their love, because it causes the gifts of divine life and of substantial Love to abound on the earth.

⁀

In the new age we are entering, the task expected of Christians is so difficult that they cannot possibly accomplish it unless there are multiplied, in the very heart of and throughout the world, constellations of spiritual energy composed of humble stars invisibly shining, each a contemplative soul given over to the life of prayer.

⁀

Without contemplative love and infused prayer, and the participation of souls given over to them in the redeeming Cross, and without the invisible support they bring to the work of all in the Mystical Body, and to that strange traffic (not lacking in irony) that Providence carries on here below, the task demanded of Christians, of all Christians, would be too heavy, and the great hope that is rising would be in vain. This hope will not be in vain, for the humble stars I am speaking of have begun secretly to glimmer; there are already more of them than one realizes, strewn across the world.

Contemplation and Prayer

⌒

For Further Reading and Reflection
Maritain Sources

On the role of the philosopher in society: *On the Use of Philosophy*, pages 3-15.

On the need for contemplation in the world: *Scholasticism and Politics*, pages 135-153; *The Peasant of the Garonne*, pages 194-253; *The Things That Are Not Caesar's*, pages 110-120.

Church Documents

On the use of contemplation and prayer to overcome tendencies toward secularism, materialism, and moral relativism: Pope John Paul II's *Ecclesia in America* (The Church in America, 1999), paragraphs 1, 7, 26-31, 43-44, 55-56, and 67-68.

~

Chapter Ten

"To Exist with the People"

Social Solidarity in a Democracy

*To exist with people means to suffer with them. For social
solidarity to exist in a democracy, citizens must be aware
of those who are suffering and be open to a charitable im-
pulse that may call for sharing in that suffering. Because
Christianity expects this from its followers, it is ideally suited
to the building of a compassionate democratic society.
Maritain was an early adherent of civil disobedience and
the work of Mahatma Gandhi and Martin Luther King,
Jr., and noted that the technique had its origins in the works
and ultimate sacrifices of the Christian martyrs. Even today, the power of Christian civil disobedience is evidenced
by the degree to which its opponents seek to suppress it.*

~

Blessed is he who suffers persecution for the sake
of the justice of God's kingdom and for the sake of

justice on earth. He suffers abuse for Christ's sake while he is abused for the sake of his brethren. Blessed is he if he is doubly persecuted. The more unhappiness he bears in his temporal existence because of his desire for justice in temporal society and because of his undertaking to "ransom the evil of the days," the more utterly and the more surely is he persecuted; and the more may he consequently hope, if he is faithful, to have in life everlasting (which for the just begins even here below) the blessedness of the persecuted; the more can he hope that his is the kingdom of Heaven.

~

Whenever we have to deal with the ingredients of human history, we are prone to consider matters from the point of view of *action* or of the *ideas* that shape action. Yet it is necessary to consider them also — and primarily from the point of view of *existence*. I mean that there is another, and more fundamental, order than that of social and political action: it is the order of communion in life, desire, and suffering. In other words, there must be recognized, as distinct from the category *to act for* or *to act with*, the category *to exist with* and *to suffer with*, which concerns a more profound order of reality.

⌒

If one loves that human and living thing which is called "the people," and which, like all human and living things is, I know, very difficult to define, but all the more real, then one's first and basic wish will be to exist with the people, to suffer with the people, and to stay in communion with the people.

⌒

If the ideas and historical trends (sometimes the worst ideas and trends) that at a certain time act upon the people are contrary to truth and to the good of man, I shall fight against them and do my utmost to change them; but I shall not, for all that, cease to exist with the people if I have once chosen so to exist.

⌒

And why should I have chosen to exist with the people? Because (speaking in religious and Christian terms) it is to the people, to the people first, that the gospel must be preached; it is the people whom Christ loved. And is it possible to evangelize those with whom one does not exist and does not suffer? What the sacred vocabulary termed "the multitudes," on whom Christ had compassion, is called "the masses" in the secular and temporal vocabulary.

☞

Clearly, every Christian individually taken is under no moral obligation to "exist with the people" in the temporal sense I am stressing at present. To posit such an obligation would be to jumble the issues and confuse the religious with the social, the spiritual with the temporal. What I am saying is that if, in a collective manner and in most instances, the social and temporal groups of Christian denomination do not exist in this way with the people, then a deep-rooted disorder is introduced into the world, and will be paid for at great cost.

☞

Imagine a political group of men who decide to resume and to transpose into the temporal order the methods of the early Christians and of apostles of all times. In cases where it becomes necessary, they carry on their campaign by voluntary suffering, they practice poverty, they endure punishment carrying the loss of civil rights. They go out to meet

these things, shouting the truth in season and out
of season, refusing in certain cases to cooperate
with the civil authority, and initiating reforms outside the law — not to disorganize the state or to im-
peril its safety, but to obtain the repeal of an unjust
law or to bear witness to the existence of a right —
to force a reform of which reason has recognized
the necessity. They prepare little by little the trans-
formation of the temporal regime, until the hour
comes when the burden of office and responsibility
shall fall into the hands of the group.

All these visible acts in the external order are for
the actors no more than occasions of spiritual trial
and adjustment in a life whose aim is the perfection
of the soul. In the achievement of these ends and in
the patient acceptance of the ill treatment they are
made to suffer, they try to be without hatred and
without pride; they exert a stern measure of self-
control so as not to be wanting in justice, and they
do not allow falsehood or anything else that degrades
man to dishonor their action; they truly love those
against whom they are fighting as they truly love
those for whom they are fighting; all the evil that
is done to them is engulfed in their charity; before

they bear witness against evil, love has consumed
the evil in their heart.

◯

Their influence on the world is great, because
by suffering injustice in cases in which the injustice
must sooner or later be avenged on earth, they
oblige the Sovereign Power, in a manner of speaking, to take their side; because their charity heaps
up on the heads of their enemies coals of fire that
cancel out ill-will or chastens it; and again because
the power of love is a radiant energy that convinces
men and carries them with it. If love is expressed in
a visible form, the radiation of this form will be out
of all proportion to its intrinsic power.

Social Solidarity in a Democracy

~

For Further Reading and Reflection
Maritain Sources

On the use of spiritual means to achieve social reforms: *Freedom in the Modern World*, pages 73-100; *On the Use of Philosophy*, pages 70-75.

On the meaning of existing with the people: *The Range of Reason*, pages 121-128.

On the Christian aspects of suffering persecution: *The Range of Reason*, pages 219-226.

Church Documents

On the reality of human suffering in the context of the Christian faith: Pope John Paul II's *Salvifici Doloris* (On the Meaning of Human Suffering, 1984), paragraphs 8, 16, 23-24, and 26-30.

Chapter Eleven

⌒

"We Are Bruised Souls"

The American Experience

For Maritain, the experience of immigrants to America reminds us that democratic evolution entails a respect both for the past and for future creative opportunities. The sufferings of past generations of immigrants to America give rise to memories, traditions, and hopes that inspire new generations.

As Christians become marginalized in secularized Western democracies, it is instructive to reflect on the methods employed by immigrant and other minority communities to thrive in a hostile society. Likewise, as it suffers indignities at the hands of the international community, America should seek to preserve the cultural and spiritual traditions that, in spite of protestations to the contrary, have so well served the world. Only in the context of the gospel does such suffering, and hope for the future, make sense.

∾

"We are bruised souls."

These words were said to me many years ago by a great American for whom I have profound respect and affection. They struck me in an indelible manner. They alluded to the wounds and sorrows of ancestors, and that memory of the sufferings caused by persecution and prejudice which they left to their progeny as a spiritual patrimony; they related to the fact that the ancestors of today's Americans were people hunted because of their religious convictions, rejected by their national community, or offended and humiliated by distress and poverty.

∾

At this point, we may grasp the hidden meaning of the basic part played by immigration in the life of this country. Each day, each year brings to the shores of America a flux of men and women who come from every part of the world and every cultural tradition, nearly broken by the moral persecutions, moral distress, or physical poverty suffered in the Old World.

They come over to commit all their remaining forces to the common task of the land of promise

that receives them. Their children will be told of
their sufferings and keep them in memory, but they
will share in the youthful force, hope, and activity
of their new national community. They will embark
on the pursuit of happiness.

☞

With respect to this basic sociological datum —
the perpetual arrival of a new first generation of
immigrants, as well as to the arrival of the first col-
onists — one might say that the tears and sufferings
of many unfortunates have been and ceaselessly are
a stream fecundating the soil of the New World and
preparing for America's grandeur.

☞

The extraordinary fact is that these tears are
not shed *in vain;* I mean with regard to the earthly
destiny of the children of man. Here lies, in my
opinion, a distinctive privilege of this country, and
a deep human mystery concealed behind its power
and prosperity. The tears and sufferings of the
persecuted and unfortunate are transmuted into a
perpetual effort to improve human destiny and to
make life bearable; they are transfigured into opti-
mism and creativity.

Christianity, Democracy, and the American Ideal

⇌

But what is the objective meaning of that
transmutation of the sufferings of the poor and the
wounded into a new strength and a new hope, if
not a Christian meaning projected into the sphere
of temporal, social, and political existence? Except
under the shade of the gospel, such a phenomenon
could neither take place nor make sense in human
history.

⇌

I spoke a moment ago of the spiritual importance of immigration for this country. Probably
immigration will pose more difficult problems in
proportion as the country becomes more populated.
It is to be hoped that that strange source of insuper-
able strength and energy which comes from the in-
flux of the poor and the humiliated, welcomed
here to live a worthy human life, will never cease
to vitalize American civilization. Without this
humble source — namely, the tears and sufferings
of the poor pouring into the flux of American life
and transmuted into human energy — America
would lose an essential ingredient of her spiritual
identity.

The supreme value in the American scale of values is *goodness;* human reliability, goodwill, devotion, helpfulness. Hence that American kindness which is so striking a feature to foreign visitors. Americans are ready to help, and happy to help. They are on equal terms of comradeship with everybody. And why? Simply because everybody is a human being. A fellowman. That's enough for him to be supposed worthy of assistance and sympathy — sometimes of exceedingly thoughtful and generous attention. When you arrive in this country, you experience in this connection a strange, unforgettable sense of relief. You breathe more easily.

From the very beginning, the European peoples dreamed of America as the Fortunate Isles, the land of promise here below. America can give them goods, food, and industrial equipment. They will take them, of course, but they will never be content with them, and never be grateful to America for them.

What they expect from America is hope. And please God that this crucial fact may never be forgotten here. It is possible to be more specific, and to say: what the world expects from America is that she keep alive, in human history, a fraternal recognition of the dignity of man — in other words, the terrestrial hope of men in the gospel.

The American Experience

⸙

For Further Reading and Reflection
Maritain Sources
On the contributions of immigrants to the American
experience: *Reflections on America*, pgs. 83-87.

Church Documents
On immigration in America: Pope John Paul II's
Ecclesia in America (The Church in America, 1999),
paragraph 65.
On immigration in Europe: his *Ecclesia in Europa* (The
Church in Europe, 2003), paragraphs 100-103.

☞

Chapter Twelve

"Kneeling Before the World"

Truth and Fellowship

Maritain was one of the first to sound the alarm over moral relativism. As the French Ambassador to the United Nations Educational, Scientific and Cultural Organiza-tion (UNESCO), he witnessed internationalists' efforts to build a global ethic to which all nations could subscribe. Unfortunately, as is the case with similar present efforts, participants adhering to a truth, such as the sanctity of hu-man life, are required to jettison their beliefs for the purpose of achieving consensus. Whether named "education for democratic citizenship," "human-rights education," or "ed-ucation for a culture of peace," these initiatives threaten to give rise to a coerced, not genuine, form of fellowship.

☞

The problem of truth and human fellowship is important for democratic societies; it seems to me to be particularly important for America, where men and women coming from a great diversity of national stocks and religious or philosophical creeds have to live together. If each of them endeavored to impose his own convictions and the truth in which he believes on all his co-citizens, would not living together become impossible? That is obviously right. Well, it is easy, too easy, to go a step further, and to ask: if each one sticks to his own convictions, will not each one endeavor to impose his own convictions on all others? So that, as a result, living together will become impossible if any citizen whatever sticks to his own convictions and believes in a given truth?

⌒

Thus, it is not unusual to meet people who think that *not to believe in any truth,* or *not to adhere firmly to any assertion as unshakably true in itself,* is a primary condition required of democratic citizens in order to be tolerant of one another and to live in peace with one another. May I say that these people are in fact the most intolerant people, for if perchance they were to believe in something as unshakably true, they would feel compelled, by the same stroke, to impose by force and coercion their own belief on their co-citizens. The only remedy they have found to get rid of their abiding tendency to fanaticism is to cut themselves off from truth.

⌒

That is a suicidal method. And it is a suicidal conception of democracy: not only would a democratic society that lived on universal skepticism condemn itself to death by starvation; but it would also enter a process of self-annihilation, from the very fact that no democratic society can live without a common practical belief in those truths which are freedom, justice, law, and the other tenets of democracy; and that any belief in these things as objectively and unshakably true, as well as in any other kind of truth, would be brought to naught by the pre-assumed law of universal skepticism.

⌒

How, then, under these circumstances, is an agreement conceivable among men assembled for the purpose of jointly accomplishing a task dealing with the future of the mind, who come from the four corners of the earth and who belong not only to different cultures and civilizations, but to different spiritual lineages and antagonistic schools of

thought? Should an agency like UNESCO throw
up the game, give up any assertion of common
views and common principles, and be satisfied only
in compiling documents, surveys, factual data, and
statistics? Or should it, on the contrary, endeavor
to establish some artificial conformity of minds, and
to define some doctrinal common denominator —
which would be likely, in the course of discussion,
to be reduced to the vanishing point?

☙

The ideological agreement that is necessary
between those who work toward making science,
culture, and education contribute to the establishment of a true peace is restricted to a certain body
of practical points and of principles of action. But
within these limits there is, and there must be, an
ideological agreement that, for all its merely practical nature, is nonetheless of major importance.

☙

Owing to the historical development of mankind, to ever-widening crises in the modern world,
and to the advance, however precarious, of moral
conscience and reflection, men have today become aware, more fully than before (although still

imperfectly) of a number of practical truths regarding their life in common upon which they can agree, but which are derived in the thought of each of them — depending upon their ideological allegiances, their philosophical and religious traditions, their cultural backgrounds, and their historical experiences — from extremely different, or even basically opposed, theoretical conceptions.

⌒

In reality, it is through rational means — that is, through persuasion, not coercion — that man is bound by his very nature to try to induce others to share in what he knows or claims to know as true and just.

⌒

I distrust any easy and comfortable friendship between believers of all denominations — I mean a friendship that is not accompanied, as it were, by a kind of compunction or soul's sorrow — just as I distrust any universalism that claims to unite in one and the same service of God, and in one and the same transcendental piety, as in some World's Fair Temple, all forms of belief and all forms of worship.

Christianity, Democracy, and the American Ideal

⪜

Let us beware of those brotherly dialogues in which everyone is in raptures while listening to the heresies, blasphemies, stuff, and nonsense of the other. They are not brotherly at all. It has never been recommended to confuse "loving" with "seeking to please."

⪜

There is, nowadays, among a good many Christians and even, without their clearly realizing it perhaps, among an alarming number of priests and consecrated people (it is these clerics, above all, whom I have in mind), a marked tendency to give efficacy primacy over truth.

⪜

The present crisis has many diverse aspects. One of the most curious spectacles it offers us is a kind of *kneeling before the world*, which is revealed in a thousand ways.

⪜

What, then, do we see around us?
In large sectors of both clergy and laity (but it is the clergy who set the example), hardly is the word

world pronounced when a gleam of ecstasy lights up the face of one and all.

⁀

That a good many Christians today kneel before the world is a fact perfectly clear. And this is what we have to look at first of all. But of what world precisely are we dealing with here? In other words, what do these Christians have in their mind; what do they think in behaving this way? This is a good deal more obscure, because, for the most part, they think very little and confusedly.

⁀

Accordingly, at least in practice and in their way of acting, and even — for those who are boldest and most determined to go the whole way — in doctrine and in their way of thinking about the world and their own religion, the great concern and the only thing that matters for them is the temporal vocation of the human race, with its march, embattled but victorious, to justice, peace, and happiness. Instead of realizing that our devotion to the temporal task must be that much firmer and more ardent, since we know that the human race will never succeed on this earth in delivering itself completely from evil — because of the wounds of Adam, and because our ultimate end is supernatural — they make of these earthly goals the truly supreme end for humanity.

In other words, there is henceforth only the earth. A complete *temporalization of Christianity*.

⸺

It is not community of race, of class, or of nation, but the love of charity that makes us what we ought to be: members of the family of God, of the only community where each person, drawn out from his fundamental loneliness, truly communicates with others and truly makes them his brothers, by giving himself to them and in a certain sense dying for them. Nothing that has ever been said points out more profoundly the mystery and dignity of the human person. Who is my neighbor? The man of my blood? Of my party? The man who does me good? No. It is the man to whom *I* show mercy, the man to whom is transmitted through me the universal gift and love of God, who makes the rain from Heaven fall upon both the good and the wicked.

⌐

For Further Reading and Reflection
Maritain Sources

On the problems associated with world government:
Man and the State, pages 188-216.

On loyalty to truth in the pursuit of human fellowship:
Ransoming the Time, pages 115-140; *Truth and Human
Fellowship*, pages 1-32.

On living as a Christian in the modern world: *The
Peasant of the Garonne*, pages 28-63.

On pursuing international cooperation: *The Range
of Reason*, pages 172-184.

Church Documents

On the proper order of relationships between individuals; individuals and public authorities; nations; and
individuals and their political communities with the
world community: Pope John XXIII's *Pacem in Terris*
(Peace on Earth, 1963), paragraphs 1-38, 80-89, 130-
141, and 161-171. See also Pope John Paul II's Janu-
ary 1, 2003 message *Pacem in Terris: A Permanent
Commitment*, his message for the celebration of the
World Day of Peace.

On the manner in which the Church can support the
building of an international community: Pope Paul
VI's *Gaudium et Spes*, paragraphs 84-90.

⌒

Chapter Thirteen

"The Chief Thing Is to Have Been Present"
Christian and Democratic Evolution

Maritain viewed as essentially complementary man's vertical movement toward eternal life and his horizontal movement through history. Since history consists of life on earth, and the corresponding presence of good and evil, for all the progress achieved in building just and loving societies, there will be setbacks. To the extent that Christianity helps its followers better live their lives, it has a positive effect on democratic evolution. Thus, democracies should never lose sight of the importance of the vertical movement, and states should do everything in their power to respect religious agencies that facilitate that movement. Hope is essential to the realization of such a Christianity-inspired civilization.

⌒

Time has a meaning and direction. Human history is made up of periods, each of which is possessed of a particular intelligible structure, and therefore of basic particular requirements. These periods are what I have proposed calling the various historical climates or historical constellations in human history.

⌒

Every great age of culture receives its deepest meaning and direction from a particular constellation of spiritual factors or dominating ideas; let us say, from a particular historical heaven. And the most significant factor to be considered in such moving appearances of the zodiac of history is the peculiar approach to God characterizing a given period of culture. What are, from this point of view, the main characteristics of the human approach to God, or of the human attitude toward God, in the new age of civilization that is emerging?

⌒

Instead of a human and rational development in continuance of the gospel, man has sought this development from pure reason *as a substitute* for the gospel. And for human life, for the concrete movement of history, this means real and very serious amputations.

☞

Prayer, evangelical virtues, suprarational truths, a sense of sin and of grace and of the gospel's beatitudes, the necessity for self-sacrifice and ascetic discipline, for contemplation, for the means of the Cross — all these have been either stuck between parentheses or finally denied. In the concrete realm of human life, reason has become divorced from the suprarational.

☞

Well, *all this simply did not work:* the unfolding of the story — of history — has shown it clearly enough. After having put aside God to become self-sufficient, man loses his soul; he seeks himself in vain, turning the universe upside down in his effort to find himself again. He finds only masks, and, behind those masks, death.

☞

The task of the emergent civilization (which will doubtless not appear tomorrow but which might possibly appear the day after tomorrow) will consist in refinding and refounding the sense of that dignity, in rehabilitating man in God and through God, not apart from God. This means a complete spiritual revolution.

☞

All the fragrance and beauty, the forms and values, the very pictures by which our ancestors lived, which made nature fraternal to them and the universe familiar, and which from generation to generation prepared us in them, have suddenly become remote and separate from us, entirely worthy of admiration and respect, but immovably fixed in what has ceased to be. This is undoubtedly the deepest cause of the great distress afflicting contemporary youth. It is strolling in its own humanity as in a museum: it sees its heart in the showcases.

☞

Christian heroism will one day become the sole solution for life's problems. Then, as God proportions His graces to human needs and tempts nobody beyond his strength, we shall doubtless see coincident with the worst condition in history a flowering of sanctity.

☞

In the perspectives of integral humanism, there must be no conflict between the vertical movement toward eternal life (begun and existing here and now) and the horizontal movement through which are revealed progressively the substance and the creative forces of man in history. Nor can there be mutual exclusion of the one by the other, for these two directions must be pursued simultaneously. And the horizontal movement of historical progression cannot be achieved well or prevented from turning to the destruction of man unless it be vitally joined to the vertical movement toward eternal life; for this horizontal movement, while it has its proper and properly temporal aims, and tends by itself to better the condition of man here below, nevertheless prepares the way, within human history, for the kingdom of God, which, for each individual person and for all humanity, is something beyond history.

Our duty is to act on history to the limit of our power: yes, but God being first served. And we must neither complain nor feel guilty if history often works against us: it will not vanquish our God, and escape His purposes, either of mercy or of justice. The chief thing, from the point of view of existence in history, is not to succeed; success

never endures. Rather, it is to *have been there*,
to have been *present*, and that is ineffaceable.

⸎

Christianity must inform or, rather, transpenetrate
the world; not that this is its principal aim (although
it is an indispensable secondary end), and not in
order that the world become right now the kingdom of God, but in order that grace may be more
and more effective in it, and in order that man
may better live there his temporal life.

⸎

I think that the task of Christian philosophy and
theology today is to give its true meaning to this mission to transform the world temporally, which up to
now has been presented in such mistaken perspectives. All I can do as an old philosopher who has already cleared the land a bit and is now at the end of
his life, is to sketch out some ideas that I believe to
be true (and, of course, some distinctions that I believe to be well founded, and terribly necessary).

⸎

What is demanded of the Christian is to *intervene* in the destiny of the world, winning at great

pains and at the risk of a thousand dangers —
through science and through social and political
action — a power over nature and a power over
history, but remaining, whatever he does, more
than ever a *subordinate* agent: servant of divine
providence and activator or "free associate" of
an evolution he does not direct as a master, and
which he also serves insofar as it develops according to the laws of nature and the laws of
history.

The Church is holy; the world is not holy.
But the world is saved in hope, and the blood of
Christ, the vivifying principle of the redemption,
acts already within it. A divine and hidden work
is being pursued in history, and in each age of
civilization, under each "historic sky," the Christian must work for a proportionate realization
(while awaiting the definitive realization of the
gospel, which is for beyond time), for a realization
of the gospel exigencies and of Christian practical
wisdom in the sociotemporal order — a realization
that is itself thwarted, in fact, and more or less
masked and deformed by sin. But that is another
matter.

☞

The evil works accumulated in time will burn
in Hell, and the good works accumulated will be
gathered into the divine barn. But pending the end,
sinners and saints will grow together. Thus, from
the point of view of the history of the kingdom of
grace, or of Christ's Mystical Body, it may be said
that two immanent movements cross each other at
each point of the evolution of mankind, and affect
each of its momentary complexes.

☞

One of these movements draws upward (toward
final salvation) everything in mankind that par-
ticipates in the divine life of the kingdom of grace,
or the Church (which is *in* the world but not *of* the
world), and follows the attraction of Christ, Head
of the human race. The other movement draws
downward (toward final doom) everything in mankind that belongs to the prince of this world, head
(as St. Thomas says) of all evildoers.

☞

It is in undergoing these two internal movements that human history advances in time. The

Christian knows that, although constantly thwarted and constantly concealed, the work of the Spirit is carried out in spite of everything, as history goes on, and that thus, from fall to fall, but also from obscure gain to obscure gain, time marches toward the resurrection.

⁂

What I have in mind is that the world (at least in the sense I just indicated) has a kind of vital unity — not political, not organized, not manifested, but real nevertheless. And by reason of this vital unity, when a history-making event, a big event for mankind, an event that carries to actuality century-old potentialities and aspirations, occurs at a particular point in space, say, in a given nation or a given people, it does not occur only for this nation or for this people, but it occurs for the world.

⁂

Now, I seem to hear somebody ask me: how can you have the face to speak of a new Christendom to come, when you see the state of our present world, with all the threats of degradation and even destruction to which mankind is being subjected, and had you not better speak of new barbarism already come?

I shall say: I believe in the possible advent of
a new Christendom because my name is Jacques.
Peter typified faith, and John charity; James typified
the second theological virtue.

I expect saints and miracle-workers to arise in
the midst of the labors of the world. Without them
I have no idea how a new Christian civilization can
ever come about.

Christian and Democratic Evolution

For Further Reading and Reflection
Maritain Sources

On the relationship between religion and culture:
Freedom in the Modern World, pages 42-72.

On the nature of a philosophy of history that acknowl-
edges the existence of God: *On the Philosophy of History*, pages 34-42.

On the presence of good and evil in the world: *On the
Philosophy of History*, pages 43-62.

On the vital unity or solidarity of the world: *On the
Philosophy of History*, pages 62-68.

On the relationship between Christianity and earthly
civilization: *Scholasticism and Politics*, pages 179-197.

On a new approach to God in culture and history: *The
Range of Reason*, pages 92-102.

Church Documents

On the role that the Church plays in the positive development of human society: Pope Paul VI's *Gaudium et
Spes* (On the Church in the Modern World, 1965),
paragraphs 1-2, 4-8, 25-26, 32-38, and 42-45.

References

The references below use abbreviations for the works listed in the bibliography. Please refer to the bibliography for complete information on each work.

Pg. 3:   Faith in the dignity . . . . FMC, 15

Pg. 4:   A person is a universe . . . . IH, 9

Pg. 4:   A single human soul . . . . RMNL, 13

Pg. 5:   The worth of the person . . . . . . RMNL, 4

Pg. 5:   Christianity confirms . . . . RT, 19

Pg. 5:   The American body politic . . . . . RA, 168

Pg. 6:   This freedom is not a celestial . . . RA, 169

Pg. 6:   This freedom leads to . . . . TC, 15

Pg. 7:   In brief, the question is to know . . . . SP, 69

Pg. 7:   Modern democracies suffer. . . . . . . SP, 70

Pg. 11:   In modern times, an attempt . . . . RR, 166

Pg. 12:   Nevertheless, I disapprove. . . . . . SRCL, 9

Pg. 12:   The very expression . . . . RR, 168

Pg. 13:   It is hard to imagine a *culture* . . . . RR, 169

Pg. 71:   Without contemplative love . . . . . PG, 83

Pg. 75:   Blessed is he who suffers . . . . RR, 221

Pg. 76:   Whenever we have to deal with . . . RR, 121

Pg. 77:   If one loves that human . . . . RR, 121

Pg. 77:   If the ideas and historical trends . . . RR, 124

Pg. 77:   And why should I have chosen . . . RR, 124

Pg. 78:   Clearly, every Christian . . . . . . RR, 125

Pg. 78:   Imagine a political group of men . . FMW, 93

Pg. 79:   All these visible acts . . . . FMW, 94

Pg. 80:   Their influence on the world . . . FMW, 94

Pg. 84:   "We are bruised souls" . . . . RA, 83

Pg. 84:   At this point, we may grasp . . . . . RA, 84

Pg. 85:   With respect to this basic . . . . . . RA, 84

Pg. 85:   The extraordinary fact . . . . RA, 85

Pg. 86:   But what is the objective meaning . . RA, 85

Pg. 86:   I spoke a moment ago . . . . RA, 86

Pg. 87:   The supreme value . . . . RA, 67

Pg. 87:   From the very beginning . . . . . . RA, 199

Pg. 91:   The problem of truth . . . . THF, 4

Pg. 92:   Thus, it is not unusual to meet . . . . THF, 4

Pg. 93:   That is a suicidal method . . . . THF, 5

Pg. 93:   How, then, under these . . . . RR, 179

Pg. 94:   The ideological agreement . . . . . . RR, 181

Pg. 94:   Owing to the historical . . . . MS, 76

Pg. 95:   In reality, it is through rational . . . THF, 7

Pg. 95:   I distrust any easy . . . . THF, 27

Pg. 96:   Let us beware of those brotherly . . . PG, 91

Pg. 96:   There is, nowadays . . . . PG, 93

Bibliography

CD   *Christianity and Democracy*. New York: Charles Scribner's Sons, 1944.

EC   *Education at the Crossroads*. New Haven: Yale University Press, 1943.

FMC   *France: My Country Through the Disaster*. New York: Longmans Green and Co., 1941.

FMW   *Freedom in the Modern World*. Notre Dame: University of Notre Dame Press, 1996.

IH   *Integral Humanism*. Notre Dame: University of Notre Dame Press, 1973.

MS   *Man and the State*. Chicago: The University of Chicago Press, 1951.

NB   *Notebooks*. Albany: Magi Books, Inc., 1984.

OUP   *On the Use of Philosophy*. Princeton: Princeton University Press, 1961.

OUPH   *On the Use of Philosophy of History*. New York: Charles Scribner's Sons, 1957.

PG   *The Peasant of the Garonne*. New York: Holt, Rinehart and Winston, 1968.

PCG	*The Person and the Common Good.* New York: Charles Scribner's Sons, 1947.
RR	*The Range of Reason.* New York: Charles Scribner's Sons, 1952.
RT	*Ransoming the Time.* New York: Charles Scribner's Sons, 1941.
RA	*Reflections on America.* New York: Charles Scribner's Sons, 1958.
RMNL	*The Rights of Man and Natural Law.* New York: Charles Scribner's Sons, 1943.
SP	*Scholasticism and Politics.* London: Geoffrey Bles, 1940; 1954.
SRCL	*Some Reflections on Culture and Liberty.* Chicago: University of Chicago Press, 1933.
TNC	*Things That Are Not Caesar's.* New York: Charles Scribner's Sons, 1931.
THF	*Truth and Human Fellowship.* Princeton: Princeton University Press, 1957.
TC	*The Twilight of Civilization.* London: Sheed and Ward, 1946.
WHB	*We Have Been Friends Together.* New York: Longmans, Green and Co., 1947.

≈

Jacques Maritain
(1882-1973)

Jacques Maritain was born on November 18, 1882, in Paris. His religious training was Protestant; his education, rationalistic and humanitarian. He attended the Lycée Henri IV (1898-1899) and the Sorbonne, where he studied modern thought in philosophy, literature, biology, and social questions. At the Sorbonne he met Raïssa Oumansoff, a Jewish Russian émigré.

While students there, Jacques and Raïssa were trained in what Maritain later referred to as "scientism," a material philosophy that sees in mathematics the universal instrument and supreme standard of knowledge. The two friends had long conversations with Felix Le Dantec, a professor in the faculty of natural sciences whose atheism and materialism left them despondent. In her book *We Have Been Friends*

Together (1942), Raïssa observed that young men who completed their philosophical studies at the Sorbonne at the beginning of the twentieth century "had no confidence in ideas except as instruments of rhetoric, and were completely unprepared for the combats of the mind and the conflicts of the world." She feared that such training would cause France to lose the battles of humanity against a barbarism that worshiped the use of force.

Unable to find the values to which they could subscribe and find meaning in life, Jacques and Raïssa agreed that, absent a near-term revelation, the solution would be suicide. They found temporary solace in the lectures of Henri Bergson, a philosopher at the Collège de France who emphasized man's ability to examine the qualitative depths of consciousness in the form of a spiritual intuition.

Abandoning their thoughts of suicide, Jacques and Raïssa married in 1904.

Shortly thereafter, they became close friends of Léon Bloy, a Catholic writer who fought against a moralistic interpretation of religion in favor of a faith energized by the contemplation of the supernatural truth revealed in the charity of Christ. Bloy was instrumental in the conversion of Jacques and Raïssa to the Catholic Church in 1906.

After passing his agrégation in philosophy in 1905, Maritain studied biology for two years at the University of Heidelberg. The Maritains returned to France in the summer of 1908, and Jacques began an intensive study of the writings of St. Thomas Aquinas.

In 1912, Maritain became professor of philosophy at the Lycée Stanislaus, although he undertook to give lectures at the Institut Catholique de Paris. He became full professor in 1921 and, in 1928, was appointed to the chair of logic and cosmology, which he held until 1939.

From 1921 to 1939, the Maritains conducted study circles for friends and acquaintances in their home and annual retreats on the application of the doctrine of St. Thomas to the problems facing modern society.

During the 1920s, Maritain was involved in a very public dispute between officials of the Catholic Church and friends and associates who were part of the Action Française political movement. Although Action Française was the most outspoken adversary of state-sponsored anticlericalism and secularism in France, Church officials strongly discouraged participation in the movement. During the dispute, which ended in 1939, Maritain published his *Things That Are Not Caesar's* (1931), the first of his writings on the relations of church and state and the role of the faithful in the pursuit of the common good.

Maritain continued his involvement in social and political issues until the beginning of World War II. In *Integral Humanism* (1936), he set forth his vision for an "integral" Christian humanism through which men could pursue their temporal political, social, and vocational callings under the full influence of their supernatural calling. Maritain became a frequent visitor to the United States and lectured annually at the Institute of Mediaeval Studies in Toronto, Canada. When war broke out at the end of 1939, he did not return to France, but taught in the United States at Princeton University (1941-1942) and Columbia University (1941-1944).

During the war, Maritain actively followed the war effort and published *France My Country Through the Disaster* (1941), a book designed (in Maritain's words) "to set down what I believe to be the real causes of the French disaster, and what I believe to be the truth about the present situation of my country." While in America, Maritain continued to lecture and publish books on the dignity and mission of the person in the face of modern society (*Scholasticism and Politics*, 1940), the philosophy of education (*Education at the Crossroads*, 1943), the natural rights of man (*The Rights of Man and Natural Law*, 1943), and the complimentary relationship between Christianity and democracy (*Christianity and Democracy*, 1945).

After the liberation of France in 1944, Maritain was named French ambassador to the Vatican, serving until 1948. He was also actively involved in drafting the United Nations Universal Declaration of Human Rights (1948) and participated in the initial meetings of the United Nations Educational, Scientific, and Cultural Organization (UNESCO). During this time, Maritain published works on the distinction between individuality and personality as they relate to the common good (*The Person and the Common Good*, 1947) and the existentialism of St. Thomas Aquinas (*Existence and the Existent*, 1947).

In the spring of 1948, Maritain returned to Princeton University as professor emeritus. He also lectured at a number of American universities, particularly at the University of Notre Dame and the University of Chicago, and frequently returned to France to lecture. While in America, Maritain published books on the need to re-establish the basic principles of democracy in the modern context (*Man and the State*, 1951), the philosophy of history (*On the Philosophy of History*, 1957), and reflections on his experiences in America (*Reflections on America*, 1958).

In 1960, Maritain and his wife returned to France. Following Raïssa's death later that year, Maritain moved to Toulouse, France, where he decided to live with a religious order, the Little Brothers of Jesus. In 1964, he published his *Moral Philosophy*, a historical and critical examination of different systems of moral philosophy. His writings on political, social, and moral philosophy influenced the discussions and Church documents produced by the Second Vatican Council, which was brought to a close on December 8, 1965. Nevertheless, in *The Peasant of the Garonne* (1968), Maritain felt compelled to critically examine certain trends within the Catholic Church since the Second Vatican Council.

Maritain died in Toulouse on April 28, 1973. He is buried alongside Raïssa in Kolbsheim (Alsace) France.

Biographical Note

⤳

James P. Kelly, III

James P. Kelly, III is President and General Counsel of Solidarity Center for Law and Justice, P.C., a religious liberty public interest law firm based in Atlanta, Georgia. He also serves as the Director of International Affairs for The Federalist Society for Law and Public Policy Studies based in Washington, D.C. Kelly represents the Federalist Society on the United States National Commission to the United Nations Educational, Scientific, and Cultural Organization. He is a graduate of the University of Georgia School of Law and resides in Alpharetta, Georgia, with his wife, Lisa, and two daughters, Kate and Caroline.

Index

L

Laity, private vows of, 43

Little teams and small flocks, 41

M

Materialism

    As a threat to democracy, 8

    As threat to freedom, 14

P

Perfection, call to, 69

Person

    Community needed by, 40

    Dignity of, 3-4

    Freedom of, 4

Persons, equality of, 5

Pluralism, 62-63

    And fellowship, 92

    Religious, 60

    Social, 53

Political parties and religion, 46

Politics

    As danger to religion, 45

    Limits of, 46

    Purpose of, 50

Progress, 108-109

Prophets needed in democracy, 28

R

Reason, limits of, 12

Religion, danger of politics to, 45

Sophia Institute Press®

Sophia Institute® is a nonprofit institution that seeks to restore man's knowledge of eternal truth, including man's knowledge of his own nature, his relation to other persons, and his relation to God. Sophia Institute Press® serves this end in numerous ways: it publishes translations of foreign works to make them accessible to English-speaking readers; it brings out-of-print books back into print; and it publishes important new books that fulfill the ideals of Sophia Institute®. These books afford readers a rich source of the enduring wisdom of mankind.

Sophia Institute Press® makes these high-quality books available to the general public by using advanced technology and by soliciting donations to subsidize its publishing costs. Your generosity can help Sophia Institute Press® to provide the public with editions of works containing the enduring wisdom of the ages. Please send your tax-deductible contribution to the address below. We also welcome your questions, comments, and suggestions.

For your free catalog, call:

Toll-free: 1-800-888-9344

or write:

Sophia Institute Press®

Box 5284

Manchester, NH 03108

or visit our website:

www.sophiainstitute.com